Learning Plains Cree and Syllabics

Animals

Carol Cardinal

Illustrated by:
Jaidence Dalpino-Severight

Learning Plains Cree and Syllabics
Copyright © 2024 by Carol Cardinal

All rights reserved. No part of this publication may be reproduced, distributed, or transmitted in any form or by any means, including photocopying, recording, or other electronic or mechanical methods, without the prior written permission of the author, except in the case of brief quotations embodied in critical reviews and certain other non-commercial uses permitted by copyright law.

Tellwell Talent
www.tellwell.ca

ISBN
978-1-77962-609-7 (Paperback)

Acknowledgements

Kinanaskomitin (Thank you), Kokum Doreen Wabasca, for sharing your knowledge with me. You helped me reclaim my language, culture and traditions. Thank you for pronouncing each word for me in this book.

Special thanks to Sandra Weller for assisting with phonics.

Kinanaskomitin, Economic Development, Chief and Council of Fort McMurray 468 First Nation for your support.

Dad for always encouraging me to follow my dreams.

My wonderful Granddaughter Jaidence you did a lovely job illustrating.

Kinanaskomitin (Thank You), Chief and Council of Fort McMurray 468 First for allowing me to borrow the star map from our Urban Office.

AMOW

(AH MOH)

BEE

ÂPISCIMÔSIS ᐊᐱᐢᒋᒧᓯᐢ
(UPS CHI MOS SIS)

DEER

ATIM
(A TIM)   ᐊᑎᒼ

DOG

KINÔSEW
(KIN O SYUE)

ᑭᓄᓭᐤ

FISH

KOHKÔS
(KOOH KOS) ᑯᐦᑯᔐ

PIG

KOHKÔSIS
(KOOH KOH SIS)

ᑯᐦᑯᓯᐢ

PIGLET

MÊSTÂCÂKANIS ᑮᐢᑕᒐᑲᓂᐢ
(MES TA CHA GAN NIS)

COYOTE

MINÔS
(MIN OSS)

ᒥᒧᐯ

CAT

MINÔSIS
(MIN OS SIS)   ᒥᓇᓯᐢ

KITTEN

MISACIMÔSIS
(MIS A CHIM MOS SIS)

COLT

MISTAHAYA
(MIS TA HIYA) ᒥᐢᑖᕽ ᐊᔭ

GRIZZLY

MISTATIM
(MIS TA TIM)
ᒥᔅᑕᑎᒼ

HORSE

MÔSWA
(MO SWA)

MOOSE

NISKA
(NIS CAH)

ᓂᐢᑲ

GOOSE

PÂHKAHÂHKWÂN ᐸᐦᑲᐦᐊᐦᑲᐧᐣ
(PA GA HA QUAN)

CHICKEN

PÂHPÂSTÊW ᐸᐦᐸᐢᑌᐤ
(PAH PAH STAYO)

LARGE WOODPECKER

PASKWÂWIMOSTOS ᐸᐢᑲᐧᐃᒧᐢᑐᐢ
(PAS KWOW MOUS TOUS)

BUFFALO

SIKÂK
(SI GAWK)

ᓯᑳᒃ

SKUNK

SÎSÎP
(SEE SEEP)

DUCK

WÂPOS
(WAH PUS)

RABBIT

www.ingramcontent.com/pod-product-compliance
Lightning Source LLC
LaVergne TN
LVHW070047070526
838200LV00028B/410